Foreword by SUMIT PAUL visiting professor at Oxford & Cambridge

RAZE THE BLAZE

"A LITTLE BIG BOOK ON FIRE SAFETY"

Foreword by **SUMIT PAUL** visiting professor at Oxford & Cambridge

RAZE THE BLAZE

"A LITTLE BIG BOOK ON FIRE SAFETY"

By

MANISH KHATANA

Worldwide Published by

Pendown Press

PENDOWN PRESS

An ISO 9001 & ISO 14001 Certified Co.,
Regd. Office: 2525/193, 1st Floor, Onkar Nagar-A,
Tri Nagar, Delhi-110035
Ph.: 09350849407, 09312235086
E-mail: info@pendownpress.com
Branch Office: 1A/2A, 20, Hari Sadan, Ansari Road,
Daryaganj, New Delhi-110002
Ph.: 011-45794768
Website: PendownPress.com

First Edition: 2020

ISBN: 978-93-90116-73-7

Layout and Cover Designed by Pendown Graphics Team
Printed and Bound in India by Thomson Press India Ltd.

CONTENTS

About Me
[Page: v-vi]
Why you should read this book?
[Page: vii-viii]

CHAPTER-1

Fire- The Necessary Evil
[Page: 1-6]

CHAPTER-2

Fire – The Places where it Hides
[Page: 7-15]

CHAPTER-3

Fire – Partners of Evil
[Page: 16-22]

CHAPTER-4

Their Attack Plans
[Page: 23-27]

CHAPTER-5

Our Counter Attack Plan
[Page: 28-31]

CHAPTER-6

Their Loss is your Gain
[Page: 32-38]

CHAPTER-7

Combat Plan
[Page: 39-46]

CHAPTER-8

Eradication of Evil
[Page: 47-48]

General Precautions
in the workplace
[Page: 49-53]

Bonus Chapter: Residential Fire
Prevention & Safety Guide

[Page: 54-67]

Conclusion

[Page: 69]

ABOUT ME

I am a Computer Engineer and equipped with an MBA degree. I am into the business of manufacturing of fire safety equipment since 2013 and with lots of research & coaching, I became a blaze protection catalyst.

My career as an entrepreneur began in 2011 when I started my company Palladium Safety Solutions Pvt. Ltd. Initially, I had started company with security services. I was running my business successfully, but one incident shook me as there was a major fire at my client's end and in just few hours, everything turned into ashes. This did not only flame the complete empire of my genuinely good customers, but also spoiled the peace and tranquility of my mind as the products of some reputed Original Equipment Manufacturers (Name can't be disclosed for privacy reasons) were of no use to extinguish fire at initial phase. From that very day, I decided to flip the coin and change the segment from security agency to a manufacturer of world-class fire safety equipments.

Ever since then, I have never failed to deliver right products with right attitude to my customers as my prime focus is to give best quality products at most competitive prices so that my dealers and distributors not only serve their respective customers with good quality products, but also earn very good margins from the deal. I firmly believe that if my clients, who are delivering good quality fire safety products, are not in the game of making one time clients but getting good referrals, they will always be in feel of abundance of orders & money in their pocket by serving the world with world class fire safety equipments.

WHY YOU SHOULD READ THIS BOOK?

We all set up our business, manufacturing units, factories, or any other industry with lots of hard work along with passion & love. Daily, we sweat equity &more than 100% effort to our business to earn good margins & build our name and fame in our industries. We prepare plans daily to develop our business to take it to the next level. We all are already above the common people as setting up a business requires lots of money, courage and foolproof strategy. Establishing a set up to provide employment to so many people can never be an easy job.

In fact, we all have been contributing to the progress of our country by manufacturing world-class products & thereby serving the world with our products. But, our dreams get doomed the day our units catch fire. Fires destroy property, cause injuries, and take lives. No matter whether it's in your own home or place of employment, educational institute, it is invariably the most dangerous stuff to our growth.

It happened in 2014 to Kalpena Industries in Dankuni, West Bengal. They had set up a packaging unit with an investment of more than 100 crore and installed latest machineries imported from Germany.

More than thousands of people were earning their bread & butter from this industry. But, one day in October 2014, the very scenario got changed. This plant turned into the ashes and brought down value of the plant from 100 crore to lakh; only that value was paid by the scrap dealers. This company couldn't be able to revive from this incident and the dreams of all the people associated with the industry, got shattered. If the proper standard operating procedures & minimum fire safety equipments could have been installed, then this(unfortunate incident) could have been avoided.

I promise you here that with this book, you would be able to avoid these types of incidents & mishappenings. The best mechanism of overcoming the fire incident is to prevent it from happening with the steps mentioned in this book as we proceed here and if any mishappening happened due to negligence, then you should have proper and minimal world-class fire safety equipments at your premises to fight with any untoward incident.

CHAPTER-1

FIRE—THE NECESSARY EVIL

> *"Fire is a good servant but a bad master; fire serves well but rules to destroy."*

Life has to essentially look out for Fire-to-strive and thrive, both! (or to live and prosper).

The fire that comes from lighting a phosphorous match today has its roots in burning the thousands years of barbarian life of early human civilization. Taming the fire opened the wings of human civilization & paved the way of transformation from age old hunters to the modern civilization. For centuries, fire has been revered as a Super Natural Power with a standard that only in its very presence, all ceremonies and rituals get proper validation. It is an integral part of everyday human needs, right from cooking, clearing land for agriculture and development, illuminating and warm dwellings to the urban industrial applications such as heating pottery, extracting ores, making alloys and much more. Fire acquired such a status due to its diverse applications just as great form of energy, that ancient cultures have regarded Fire as God.

However, Fire has a burning negativity too!!

It has the power to consume everything that exists and this makes it a necessary evil.

Fire has the power to burn materials around, impact the environment and cause deep losses to life. In anger, it engulfs belongings, present and future. Even the heat and smoke that originates from fire, potentially damage and destroy causing injuries, panic and chaos.

Our Nation has faced 1.6 million fires in 2017 with 27,027 deaths as per a research conducted by Global Disease Burden that recently published a 195-nation analysis in The BMJ Injury Prevention Journal.

Commercial Spaces, Malls, Congested areas, factories, industries, warehouses, work offices and residential spaces, nothing can escape the wrath of this Giant.

And the damage that this Inferno causes is unbearable— physically, mentally, economically and otherwise. Even if its impact can be diluted or healed, the Loss and the Scars remain.

Typically, fire comes from a chemical reaction between oxygen in the atmosphere and some sort of fuel (wood or gasoline, for example). Of course, wood and gasoline don't spontaneously catch fire just because they're surrounded by oxygen. For the combustion reaction to happen, you have to heat the fuel till its ignition temperature. For Example wood can be burnt if its temperature reaches to 150 degree Celsius. Every substance has got its burning temperature, and once the heat reaches to the corresponding temperature, a certain product catches fire.

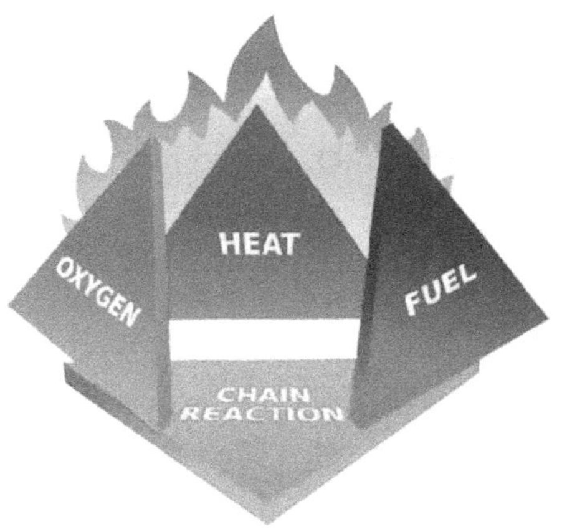

(FIRE TRIANGLE)

Fire can be extinguished by removing any one of the elements of the fire tetrahedron. Consider a natural gas flame, such as from a stove-top burner. The fire can be extinguished by any of the following means:

1) Turning off the gas supply, which removes the fuel source;

2) Covering the flame completely, which smothers the flame and the available oxidizer (the oxygen in the air) and displaces it from the area around the flame with CO2;

3) Application of water, which removes heat from the fire faster than the fire can produce it (similarly, blowing hard on a flame will displace the heat of the currently burning gas from its fuel source, to the same end), or

4) Application of a retardant chemical such as Halon to the flame, which retards the chemical reaction itself until the rate of combustion is too slow to maintain the chain reaction.

Stages of Fire

By most standards, there are 4 stages of a fire. These stages are incipient, growth, fully developed, and decay. The following is a brief overview of each stage.

Incipient

This first stage begins when heat, oxygen and a fuel source combine and have a chemical reaction resulting in fire. This is also known as "ignition" and is usually represented by a very small fire which often (and hopefully) goes out on its own, before the following stages are reached. Recognizing a fire in this stage provides you thebest chance of suppression or escape.

Growth

The growth stage is where the structures fire load and oxygen are used as fuel for the fire. There are numerous factors affecting the growth stage including where the fire started, what combustibles are near it, ceiling height and the potential for "thermal layering". It is during the shortest of the 4 stages when a deadly "flashover" can occur; potentially trapping, injuring or killing firefighters.

Fully Developed

When the growth stage reaches its max. and all combustible materials get ignited, that fire is considered fully developed. This is the hottest phase of a fire, and hence the most dangerous for anybody trapped within.

Decay

Usually the longest stage of a fire, the decay stage is characterized by a significant decrease in oxygen or fuel, putting an end to the fire. Two common dangers during this stage are– first the existence of non-flaming combustibles, which can potentially start a new fire if not fully extinguished and second, there is the danger of a back draft when oxygen is reintroduced to a volatile, confined space.

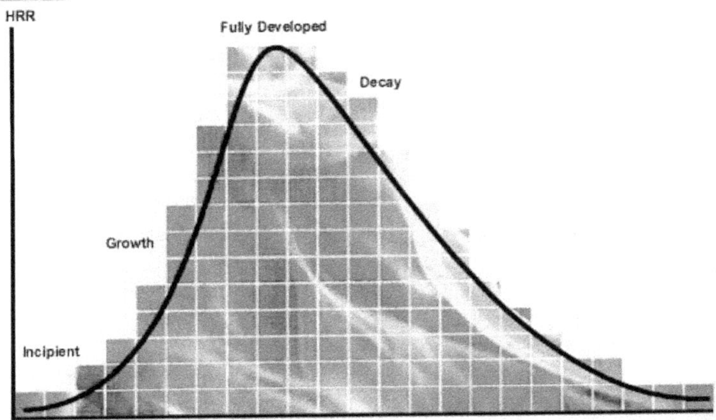
Heat Release Rate (HRR) and Fire Development
HRR
Fully Developed
Decay
Growth
Incipient
Time

CHAPTER-2

FIRE—THE PLACES WHERE IT HIDES

"Flattery and hypocrisy taste sweet but hide sizzling fire within, capable of robbing the peace of Life."

Bad Master hides its vices none other than within weak servants!

As a Monster fears danger to go to public usually, so is the Fire Dragon!

Like, life's hidden burning points such as sarcasm, hypocrisy, flattery simmers, fire just waits for its show within our homes and offices.

Low-grade electrical wire behind the walls, unattended candles or isolated stoves with ill-placed flammable items around, dryers with lint trapped deep inside the vent or the tube, loose electrical outlets, smoke detectors with old batteries are everyday casual things that we refuse to consider them as cause of fire. Old appliances with damaged wiring such as toasters, fans, lamps and other appliances which need urgent repair, can also lead to fire.

A simple and common example opens the scene in a better way. How many of you have noticed that a building undergoing renovation usually has floating Sawdust? As it burns fast, it is a great source of hidden calamity. Cigarettes, fire place that has not been cleaned for a long time, chimneys, ground heaters within three feet of flammable objects, are also safe places for Fire to emerge.

Stowing the land mowers away before they have cooled down, unattended burner on high flame also waits for Fire in residential areas.

In industries, factories and warehouses storage of combustible material, flammable liquids and vapours, built up of dust, faulty electrical appliances and equipment, overloading of power sockets and reckless human errors are enough to summon Fire.

Drop ceilings, attics, electrical boxes embedded inside walls are secret places where this rogue—Fire hides. Obviously, it is not visible from outside but as the right time arrives (for a wrong step), smoke or burning odour marks the presence of their vicious master.

The threat of fire can never be turned down without locating the real culprit. The damage is all yours and forever!

Causes of Fire

Here are four most common causes of fires and explosions:

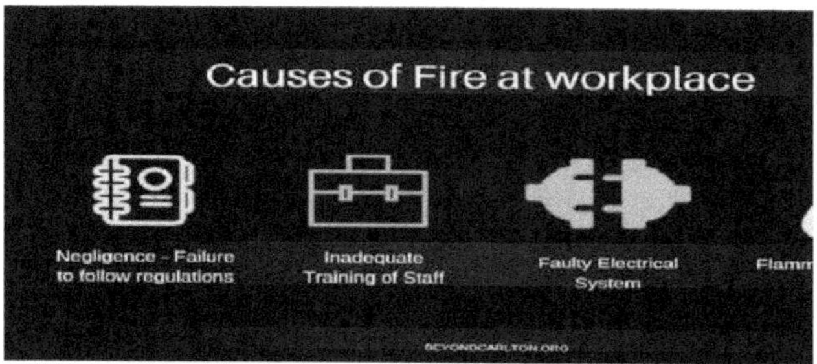

Negligence or Human Error

The major reason for fire inside the workplace is basic human error, which is typically because of incidents that were not intentional. A number of things can happen in a variety of ways including burning food in a staff area, spilling flammable liquids, improper use of machinery or equipment that overheats, and simple carelessness. Sadly, there are plenty of opportunities for fire to start at work due to the negligence and lack of care.

Another reason of negligence is observed for an attempt to get a task done quicker; short cuts have been known to be taken where certain workers have chosen to ignore correct procedures to get the job done faster, which could indirectly cause a major fire and health and safety risk. Example being the blocking of ventilation areas, stacking paper or card in a flammable area, misusing or improperly storing flammable or combustible materials, or overusing equipment or using equipment improperly.

One method to prevent these types of incidents from escalating is to ensure that there's plenty of suitable fire extinguishers and other fire safety equipments around the work area which we will discuss later on as we proceed in upcoming chapters. Business owners should conduct reviews, retraining and assessments at regular intervals to ensure proper workmanship and reduce any risk of fire in the future.

Inadequate Training of Staff

This is the most common cause of causalities & even fire incidents, as people are unaware of the standard safety operating procedures in their office or even at home. Accidental outbreaks of fire can cause a serious damage to life as well as assets. Ensuring a fail-proof plan, especially in a workplace is important for employees as well as employers. Fire destroys property, causes injuries, and takes lives. A fire in the workplace can also mean the termination of jobs, as many of the offices and factories destroyed by fire in INDIA are never rebuilt. One of the key strategies to maintaining a safe workplace and preventing fires is fire- safety training.

With proper training, workers can eliminate fire hazards and respond quickly and efficiently if a fire breaks out, whereas without proper training, even a small lapse can quickly grow into a major accident with devastating outcomes.

Everyone is at risk if there is a fire. However, there are some workers who may be at greater risk due to their vulnerability with fire at work, or because they're not familiar with the premises or the equipments at their work site.

Fire safety training can teach workers how to recognize fire hazards, conduct a fire safety risk assessment, prevent a workplace fire, and respond if a fire occurs. You will be getting enough knowledge in this book to train the people at your respective workplace about the vulnerability with fire and how to get protection if fire occurs.

So, I would like to conclude here that everyone is responsible for preventing fires in the workplace–employers and employees alike. In addition to possible injury and loss of life, a massive fire can close down a workplace resulting in significant job losses. However, it is possible to minimize the threat of fire to people and property by teaching everyone to work together to prevent fire with comprehensive fire safety training.

Faulty Electrical System/Wiring

A failure or malfunction within the electrical components of equipment or machinery can cause electrical fire. Electrical fire originates in electric wires, cables, circuit breakers, and within electrical components. Fire starts in electrical panels from overloaded circuits or age of the panel.

Outdated electrical wiring often causes electrical fires. If a home or office is over 20 years' old, or even of less-than-a-decade, may not have the wiring capacity to handle the increased amount of electrical appliances in today's average home, such as computers, wide-screen televisions, video players, microwaves and air conditioners.

The outdated wiring cannot handle the increased power load. These wiring tend to heat up quickly, and hence catch fire.

Sometimes it's hard to tell if you have old and unsafe wiring because electrical work is mostly hidden behind the walls. Remember, wiring problems are a major fire threat. Pay attention to the following signs of hidden electrical issues:

- Frequently overloaded circuit breakers
- Flickering lights or intermittent power outages

- Appliances or electrical devices that feel excessively hot
- Shocks or sparks from appliances or outlets
- Unexplained burning smells

If you see frayed electrical cords, get them replaced immediately by an electrician. These exposed cords, that run along your floor or in your walls, can be incredibly dangerous if they spit out a spark.

Electrical fires are among the most dangerous forms of combustion due to which they can spread quickly and grow out of control. By following the standards as discussed in this book, you will get the help to reduce the chances of an electrical fire.

Flammable Material

Flammable materials are the ones that are ignited or flame immediately when contacting with fire or high temperature in the air and continue to burn or slightly flame when leaving fire, such as plywood, fibreboard, chemicals, wood and foil. Generally speaking, flammable material will ignite (catch on fire) and burn easily at normal working temperatures. Combustible materials have the ability to burn at temperatures that are usually above working temperatures.

There are several specific technical criteria and test methods for identifying flammable and combustible material. Flammable and combustible materials are present in almost every workplace. Fuels and many common products like solvents, thinners, cleaners, adhesives, paints, waxes and polishes may be flammable or combustible liquids. Everyone who works with these liquids, must be aware of their hazards and how to work safely with them.

Flammable and combustible liquids themselves do not burn. It is the mixture of their vapours and air that burns. Gasoline, with a flashpoint of -40°C (-40°F), is a flammable liquid. Even at temperatures as low as -40°C (-40°F), it gives off enough vapour to form a burnable mixture in air. Phenol is a combustible liquid. It has a flashpoint of 79°C (175°F), so it must be heated above that temperature before it can be ignited in air.

Each year people are injured at work by flammable substances accidentally catching fire or exploding. Work which involves using or creating chemicals, vapours, liquids, gases, solids or dusts that can readily burn or explode, is considered hazardous.

The effects of an explosion or a fire in the workplace can be devastating in terms of the lives lost, injuries, significant damage to property and the environment, and to the business community.

Most fire are preventable. Fire safety is important and those responsible for workplaces and other non-domestic premises to which the public have access, can avoid them by taking responsibility for and adopting fire-safe behaviour and procedures.

So, as we proceed in the book, you will get the standard operating procedures to overcome these concerns at your workplace.

CHAPTER–3

FIRE–PARTNERS OF EVIL

"Thoughts are the fuel that burns the fire of Life within the heart and soul."

Evil plans but not without the aid of accomplices! Dangerously potent accomplices in homes aid their Master to serve his ulterior purposes. Don't be fooled by their appearance and names—nail polish, nail polish remover, rubbing alcohol, aerosol cans, linseed oil, gasoline, paint thinner, turpentine, non-dairy creamers to name a few. As they feel the presence of Master, they get ignited. To support them, home furnishings, rubber items and plastic decorative shake hands with them. Even the Hand Sanitizer proves its loyalty with much enthusiasm as it burns brighter.

Besides, there are other accomplices in the form of inflammable materials present in industries and well-settled in warehouses. Their role is to spread the kingdom of Fire. Blasting caps, igniters, fireworks, fuses, ammunition and flares are blasting agents and explosives elevate fire with release of gas and heat. Even pocket lighters, blow torches and Aerosols or gases dissolved in solvents are great fire partners. Liquids such as cleaning compounds, petroleum, paint removers, benzene, acetone etc. happily gel with Fire for more impact.

These accomplices act as partners in crime that not only help to start a fire, but also burn rapidly to propagate fire.

Evil Partners at Work Place

1. Combustible dust

Often overlooked, and highly deadly, combustible dust is a major cause of fire in food manufacturing, wood working, chemical manufacturing, metal working, pharmaceuticals, and just any industry you can name. The reason is that everything, including food, dyes, chemicals, and metals—even materials that aren't fire risks in larger pieces—has the potential to be combustible in dust form.

And these explosions aren't easy to contain. In the typical incident, a small fire will result from combustible material coming into contact with an ignition source. This may be a dust explosion, but it doesn't have to be. In fact, it could be any other type of explosion on this list.

However, this small explosion isn't the problem. The problem is what happens next. If there's dust in the area, the primary explosion will cause that dust to become airborne. Then, the dust cloud itself can ignite, causing a secondary explosion that can be of many times the size and severity of the primary explosion. If enough dust has accumulated, these secondary explosions have the potential to bring down entire facilities, causing immense damage and fatalities.

2. Hot work

Hot work is one of the leading causes of industrial fires across all industries.

Although hot work is commonly equated with welding and torch cutting, there are many other activities—including brazing, burning, heating, and soldering—that pose a fire hazard. This is because the sparks and molten material, which reach temperatures greater than 1000°F, can easily travel more than 35 feet.

Hot work is also a major culprit in combustible dust fires, as the sparks generated from the work can ignite dust in the surrounding area.

In one of the incidents, three contract welders were seriously burned when sparks ignited the wood dust in the silo where they were working. The investigation found a trifecta of problems: the silo hadn't been cleaned of dust before the work began, no hot work permit had been issued, and there was no fire protection and prevention plan in place.

3. Flammable liquids and gasses

Flammable and combustible materials are present in almost every workplace. Fuels and many common products like solvents, thinners, cleaners, adhesives, paints, waxes and polishes may be flammable or combustible liquids. Everyone who works with these liquids, must be aware of their hazards and how to work safely with them.

These fires, which often occur at chemical plants, can be disastrous.

4. Equipment and machinery

Faulty equipment and machinery are also major causes of industrial fires.

Heating and hot work equipment are typically the biggest problems here—in particular, furnaces that aren't properly installed, operated, and maintained. In addition, any mechanical equipment can become a fire hazard because of friction between the moving parts. This risk can be brought down to practically zero, simply by following recommended cleaning and maintenance procedures, including lubrication.

What may surprise you is that even seemingly innocuous equipment can be a hazard under certain circumstances. And, in many cases, the equipment is least likely to be thought of as a fire risk turns out to be the biggest problem. This is because companies may not recognize the risk and therefore won't take the necessary precautions.

5. Electrical hazards

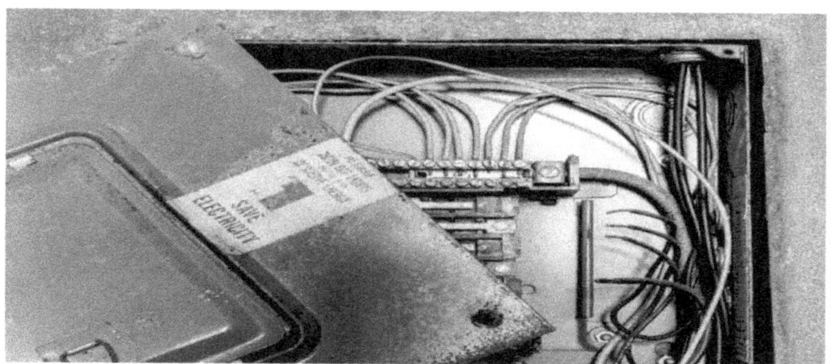

Electrical fires are one of the top five causes of fires in manufacturing plants. Here is a non-exhaustive list of specific electrical hazards:

- Wiring that is exposed or not up to code

- Overloaded outlets

- Extension cords
- Overloaded circuits
- Static discharge

The damage caused by these fires can quickly compound, thanks to several of the other items on this list. Any of the above hazards can cause a spark, which can serve as an ignition source for combustible dust, as well as flammable liquids and gasses.

CHAPTER–4

THEIR ATTACK PLANS

When Evil attacks, it plans to add
everything around; whether bad or good!

When common flammable liquids, gases or solids present in households or work spaces ignite and begin large fires; their vapours travel and spread in air to highlight fire.

They come together with a source of ignition and involve oxygen to raise fire and attack your premises with newly- acquired energy.

Ignition may come from open flame, sparking, lit cigarette or a chemical reaction. But, they need goodness of Oxygen to execute their vicious attack plan. They turn life-giving fuel–Oxygen to be an essential part of their destruction game. For this, oxidizers such as potassium permanganate, potassium chlorate, chlorine dioxide and chlorine supply oxygen to initiate fire.

All the accomplices of fire understand the importance of Oxygen, so they influence it to have it. Together they craft a devastating plan and involve other elements of space to cause havoc.

Resultant-Spreading from air-vents or furnaces, they cause severe damage. They have a dark plan, to attack, hurt and conquer.

You need a perfect defense, for they are here to consume or die.

Steps to prevent fire in combustible dust & hot work incidents

Like combustible dust incidents, hot work disasters are preventable by the following proper safety procedures:

- **Avoid hot work if possible.** This isn't always a feasible solution, but if there's an alternative, take it.

- **Train personnel** on the hazards associated with hot work, any site-specific hazards, the proper policies and procedures, and the use of safety equipment.

- **Ensure that the area is clear of flammable or combustible materials** including dusts, liquids, and gasses.

- **Use a written permit system** for all hot work projects, even where permits aren't required. Better safe than sorry!

- **Supervise the work.** Especially if you use outside contractors, make sure that a safety professional is on hand to provide supervision.

Steps to prevent flammable liquid and gas incidents

There is certainly some danger inherent in any work involving flammable liquids and gasses, but all available safety precautions should be taken to mitigate these risks.

- **Know the hazards.** One major component of prevention is simply knowing the safety information for every liquid on your premises. This information is available on the Material Safety Data Sheet (MSDS) that comes with such products.

- **Store flammable liquids properly.** Make sure that all hazardous materials are stored according to OSHA-compliant procedures.

- **Control all ignition sources.** Except when you're intentionally heating the flammable materials, keep ignition sources as far from them as possible.

- **Provide personal protective equipment.** This is a must across all categories of fire hazards, especially when liquids and gasses are involved.

- These resources from the U.S. and Canadian federal governments provide more information about how to stay safe and compliant:

Steps to prevent equipment and machinery incidents

Strategies for preventing fires due to equipment and machinery issues fall into three main categories:

- Awareness
- Cleaning and housekeeping
- Maintenance

Awareness

You can't prevent risks you don't know exist, nor can your employees. Provide safety awareness training so that everyone in your facility knows what risks to watch out for and what to do if they find one.

Cleaning and Housekeeping

Keep your equipment and machinery—and the area surrounding it—clean. Equipment, especially electrical equipment that is covered with dirt or grease poses a huge risk. By keeping your equipment and machinery clean, you'll up your chances that, should a fire start, it won't have enough fuel available to burn for long.

Maintenance

Finally, follow the manufacturer's recommended maintenance procedures for all the equipments and machineries in your plant. In addition to reducing your fire risk by preventing overheating, regular maintenance will also keep your equipment working in tip-top shape.

Steps to prevent electrical fire incidents

As with the previous risks, the key to preventing electrical fires is awareness and prevention. This involves training, maintenance, and best practices. Here are a few to put into practice right now:

- Don't overload electrical equipment or circuits.
- Don't leave temporary equipment plugged in when it's not in use.
- Avoid using extension cords, and never consider them permanent solutions.
- Use antistatic equipment where required by NFPA or OSHA.
- Follow a regular housekeeping plan to remove combustible dust and other hazardous materials from the areas that contain equipment and machinery.
- Implement a reporting system so that anyone who observes an electrical fire risk, can report it without consequences.

CHAPTER–5

OUR COUNTER ATTACK PLAN

Remember, counter attack is the best defense when the battle become- Do or Die!

8 Fire Safety Tips for Office or any other Commercial Buildings

Safety Tips

Protecting your facility and employees against fire breakouts is crucial. Real estate agents and business owners should be aware of fire prevention issues and measures that are needed to reduce the risks. If fire strikes your commercial building, it can cause big losses. Therefore, it is good to be vigilant. This guide provides 8 essential fire prevention tips for commercial properties:

1. **Educate your Employees about Fire Safety:** You should enlighten your employees about fire safety to protect them and your commercial building. For

instance, you need to show them the exit doors in case of a fire breakout. Additionally, you should tell them to keep all the working equipments in proper order to minimise risks.

2. **Install Automatic Sprinkler Systems and Fire Extinguishers:** You should purchase high-quality fire extinguishers and sprinkler systems and install them on your commercial property. After buying them, you should hire an experienced contractor to install them and educate your staff members on how to use them in case fire strikes your building.

3. **Strictly Enforce No Smoking Policies:** Whether you deal with flammable equipment in the workplace or not, you should enforce strict smoking policies. Employees caught smoking at work should face high penalties to discourage the act. You should put no smoking signs at the entry points to warn visitors and other people against smoking in your compound.

4. **Do not Store Unnecessary Combustible Materials in your Commercial Buildings:** In order to minimize the risks of fire breakouts, it is advisable to keep flammable items away from your commercial property. You need to keep your commercial building clean and orderly all the time.

5. **Install Smoke Alarms and Detectors:** Smoke detectors and alarms will notify you immediately as and when fire strikes your building. These measures will give you an opportunity to put the fire off before spreading and damaging everything. You need to buy this equipment from authorized dealers in your locality to enhance efficiency.

6. **Check your Fire Alarms/Detections Regularly:** After installing smoke detectors, alarms, and other equipments, you need to check them regularly to enhance efficiency. It is advisable to ensure that they are functioning well all the time to avoid inconveniences in case of a fire breakout. If they have broken down, you should hire an expert to fix them.

7. **Be in Touch with the Local Fire Department:** You can invite your local fire department to pay a visit to your facility and check your fire prevention measures. They will give you their opinions and guide you to make improvements where necessary. Additionally, in case fire strike in your commercial building, they will arrive on time and put it off before causing massive damages.

8. **Maintain your Electrical Systems and Appliances:** Poorly maintained electrical systems and appliances can cause fire. Therefore, it is advisable to check their efficiency regularly. You

should replace the old and worn out appliances with modern ones to save electrical energy and minimize the risks of fire breakout.

In a nutshell, on your free time, you should check the condition of your building and electrical connections. Proper monitoring of your property will enable you to detect problems that can cause fire early and hire a professional to fix them.

CHAPTER–6

THEIR LOSS IS YOUR GAIN

*In a battle, whatever be the
case, you must be ready to Win!*

Preparation is prevention intelligence. Once you are prepared, your soul takes up your role. A fight with proper planning, precautions, counter attack etc. can ensure your safety in the event of Fire. Whether it is your workplace or home, you should always be Fire Ready.

9 Easy Ways to Improve Safety in a Work Environment

Here are 10 quick and easy tips for a safer manufacturing workplace.

1. Inform Supervisors of Unsafe Conditions

If you see something that could potentially hurt someone, remove the object or clean the area if you can do safely. Otherwise, inform your supervisor. Since your supervisor is legally obligated to keep you and your fellow employees' working environment is safe, he/she must take action.

2. Use Equipment, Machines, and Tools Properly

Misusing tools and machines is the most prevalent cause of workplace injuries. When using equipment, make sure that you are using each piece of equipment for its intended purpose, and more importantly using it correctly. Furthermore, regularly clean and inspect equipment to ensure that it is safe.

3. Wear Safety Equipment (PPE)

When cleaning up messes and using equipment, make sure that you have the proper safety equipment. Make sure that you wear the proper safety equipment and check that your safety equipment is undamaged, significantly lowers your likelihood of getting injured.

4. Prevent Slips and Trips

As the second most prevalent cause of non-fatal occupational injuries, it is vital to ensure that aisles are clear and spills are cleaned to prevent employees from tripping or slipping. If you are dealing with a liquid, use drip pans and guards. Clean up any spills immediately to keep conditions safe. Also, check your workplace to make sure that there are no holes, loose boards, or nails projecting from the floor. If any of these characteristics exist, replace the damaged flooring. In areas that cannot easily be cleaned, consider installing anti-slip flooring.

5. Keep Work Areas and Emergency Exits Clear

Make sure to remove any clutter blocking emergency exits, equipment shutoffs, and areas that you are working. A cluttered work area can lead to not having enough space to use tools and pick up heavy objects properly. Furthermore, if an exit is obstructed, you may not be able to quickly escape if an emergency occurs. Placing equipment in proper storage areas after use will help keep the work area and emergency exits clear.

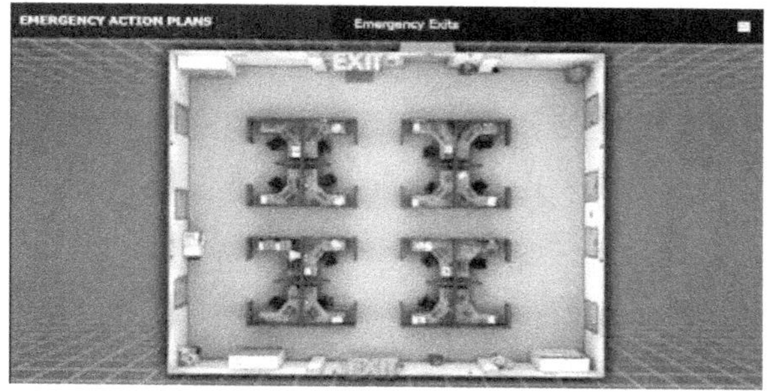

6. Eliminate Fire Hazards

If you are using combustible materials in the work environment, only keep the amount you need for the task at hand. When you are not using the flammable material, store the chemical in an assigned safe storage area away from sources of ignition. Also, store combustible waste in metal receptacles and dispose it of daily.

5 percent or more of a room's surface being covered at 0.8 millimetres of dust—about the width of a dime—can cause an explosion if the dust catches fire. To prevent dust accumulation, use industrial vacuums to frequently clean areas where dust gathers.

7. Avoid Tracking Hazardous Materials

To ensure that hazardous materials are not accidentally tracked into other areas, make sure that work area mats are maintained and kept clean. Prevent cross-contamination by using different cleaning materials—such as mops—for various spills, and change clothes if you spill toxic materials on them. Also, if you work with toxic materials, do not wear your work clothes athome.

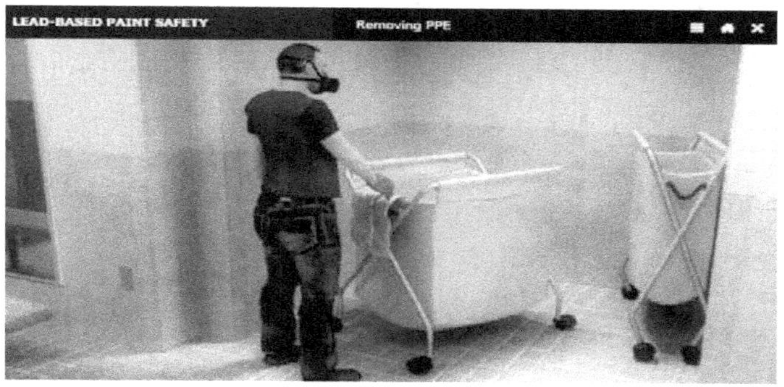

8. Prevent Objects from Falling

To keep objects from falling, use protections such as nets, toe boards, and toe rails. In addition, stack boxes straight up and down, and place heavy objects on lower shelves. Furthermore, keep stacked objects out of the way of aisles and work areas.

9.   Use Correct Posture when Lifting

To avoid injuring your back when you are trying to pick up an item, keep your back straight, use your legs to lift, and pick up the item without stooping or twisting. Whenever possible, use mechanical aids such as a conveyor belt, wheelbarrow, or forklift.

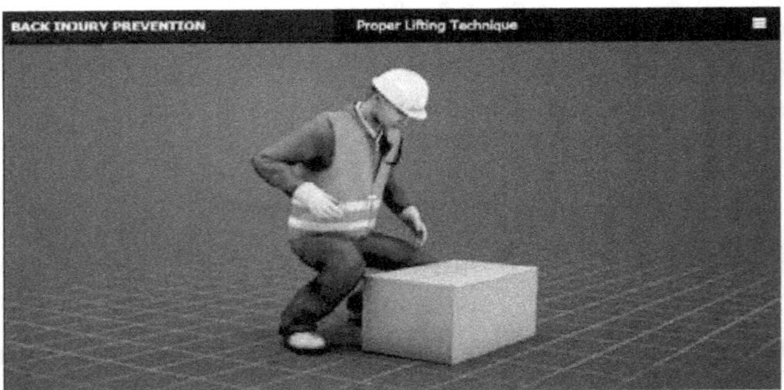

CHAPTER 7

COMBAT PLAN

> *"Many times Life does not give a second chance, all you have is now to respond or you will perish, just like when the Evil strikes, response time make all the difference in saving or losing people and property."*

When Fire spreads, it can often become uncontrollable and cause lots of damage. Quick response can save Life and restrict the devastation. Everyone involved, such as the staff, must know beforehand as to what to do understand their role and work in sync with others to ensure that the fire does not spread.

The Emergency Plan of the building must be thorough and well understood by all. Everyone must know the designated area where they must gather and what to do in case anyone comes across smoke or heat. Activating the fire alarm for others to be warned should be on top priority and you must know how to do that.

Employees and workers must know how to use a portable fire extinguisher that can stop small fires that are limited. However, not all fire extinguishers are suitable for electrical or grease fires and you must know the functionality of yours.

Also, large fires that are spreading or blocking escape routes cannot be fought easily and you should not try to fight these, but instead try to move yourself and others to safe places and call for help by dialing Fire Emergency Number 1-0-1.

The rival is dangerous and marching. It is time for Action.

You have to not only block its way but also provide safety to your loved ones.

Basic Fire Safety Equipments Required to Keep Place Safe & Secure

Every business is different but there are some key pieces of fire safety equipment that every organization needs whether they are in an office environment, a warehouse or a factory.

A. FIRE ALARM SYSTEMS

Fire alarms are essential for every building in a business and should be tested weekly. There are wide range of fire alarm systems, both battery and mains power operated. Visual alarms are also extremely useful for warehouses and factories as they offer a dual warning with the use of red led technology as well as an audible alarm to draw the attention of all employees in its range.

B. FIRE EXIT SIGNS

Fire exit signs are essential for all businesses to guide users to the correct exit. Fire depot supply emergency exit boxes and exit hanging signs which use long life LED's for maximum durability in the case of a fire.

C. EMERGENCY LIGHTING

During a fire, there is an increased risk of the main power supply cutting out which means emergency lighting is necessary for employees and customers to exit safely. The emergency lights provided by fire depot will operate in emergency mode for up to 3 hours.

D. GENERAL FIRE FIGHTING EQUIPMENT

Firefighting systems and equipment vary depending on the age, size, use and type of building construction. A building may contain some or all of the following features:

(1) Fire Extinguishers

(2) Fire Hose Reels

(3) Fire Hydrant Systems

(4) Automatic Sprinkler Systems

1. Fire Extinguishers

Fire extinguishers are provided for a 'first attack' firefighting measure, generally undertaken by the occupants of the building before the fire service arrives. It is important that occupants are familiar with extinguisher type to use in case of fire.

Most fire start as a small fire and may be extinguished if the correct type and amount of extinguishing agent is applied whilst the fire is small and controllable.

The Principle Fire Extinguisher Include

Extinguishing Agent	Principle Use
Water	Wood and paper fires not electrical
Foam	Flammable liquid fires like petrol, diesel or kerosene not electrical
Carbon dioxide	Electrical fires
Dry Chemical (ABC Type)	Wood, Paper, Flammable liquids and electrical fires
Wet chemical	Fat/Cooking oil fires - not electrical
Special Purpose	Various (e.g. metal fires)
Clean Agent	Server room, Expensive machinery, Wood, Paper, Flammable liquids and electrical fires

Fire extinguisher locations must be clearly identified. Extinguishers are colour coded according to the extinguishing agent.

It is the policy of the community safety and resilience department that fire extinguishers be logically grouped at exits from the building, so that occupants first go to the exit and then return to fight the fire, knowing that a safe exit lies behind them, away from the fire. In some instances, this will be at odds with the prescriptive requirements of Indian Standards of IS CODE 15683 portable fire extinguishers and fire blankets selection and location, which simply specify a distance of travel to a fire extinguisher rather than their location in relation to escape paths. Blind compliance with the standard has the potential to place the fire between the occupant and the safe escape path.

2. Fire Hose Reels

Fire hose reels are provided for use by occupants as a 'first attack' firefighting measure but may, in some instances, also be used by firefighters.

When stowing a fire hose reel, it is important to first attach the nozzle end to the hose reel valve, then close the hose reel valve, then open the nozzle to relieve any pressure in the wound hose, then close the nozzle. This achieves two principle objectives:

- A depressurised hose and hose reel seal will last longer if permanently pressurised.

- When the hose reel is next used, the operator will be forced to turn on the isolating valve, thus charging the hose reel with pressurised water supply, before being able to drag the hose to the fire. A potential danger exists if the operator reaches the fire and finds that no water is available because the hose reel valve is still closed.

  Because hose reels are generally located next to an exit, in an emergency it is possible to reach a safe place simply by following the hose.

3. Fire Hydrant Systems

Fire hydrant systems are installed in buildings to help firefighters quickly attack the fire. Essentially, a hydrant system is a water reticulation system used to transport water in order to limit the amount of hose that firefighters have to lay, thus speeding up the firefighting process.

Fire hydrants are for the sole use of trained firefighters (which includes factory firefighting teams). Because of the high pressures available, serious injury can occur if untrained persons attempt to operate the equipment connected to such installations.

Fire hydrant systems sometimes include ancillary parts essential to their effective operation such as pumps, tanks and fire service booster connections. These systems must be maintained and regularly tested, if they are to be effective when needed.

The placement of such equipment needs to closely interface with fire service operational procedure; simply complying with demand to satisfy code provisions is a potential recipe for disaster.

Fire hydrant system includes the following:

- Hydrants
- Hosebox
- Rrl hosepipes
- Branch pipe

4. Automatic Sprinkler Systems

Time is essential in the control of fire. Automatic sprinkler systems are one of the most reliable methods available for controlling fires. Today's automatic fire sprinkler systems offer state of the art protection of life and property from the effects of fire. Sprinkler heads are now available which are twenty times more sensitive to fire than they were ten years ago.

A sprinkler head is really an automatic (open once only) tap. The sprinkler head is connected to a pressurised water system. When the fire heats up the sprinkler head, it opens at a pre-set temperature, thus allowing pressurised water to be sprayed both down onto the fire and also up to cool the hot smoky layer and the building structure above the fire. This spray also wets combustible material in the vicinity of the fire, making it difficult to ignite, thereby slowing down or preventing fire spread.

When a sprinkler head operates, the water pressure in the system drops, activating an alarm, which often automatically calls the fire service via a telephone connection.

Some people say sprinklers cause a lot of water damage. As has been explained, only those sprinkler heads heated by the fire operate; all sprinklers in a building do not operate at once. Usually non-fire water damage only occurs if the occupants carelessly damage the system. Firefighters use much more water than a sprinkler system; the combined damage from a fire and the water used by firefighters dramatically.

Because, historically, complete extinguishment of fires has not been achieved. It is traditional to consider that sprinklers only control fire growth until intervention occurs by the fire service. Today, some sprinkler systems are designed for early suppression and are considered to have failed if they do not extinguish the fire.

E. FIRE BLANKETS

No kitchen area is complete without a fire blanket to smother flames, should the need arise. Available in a range of sizes and in either a hard or soft case, the blanket is accessed simply by pulling on the Velcro strips.

CHAPTER–8

ERADICATION OF EVIL

With Knowledge, all evils
ward off!

Knowledge is the greatest asset in **Life. Knowing** your own skills and the weaknesses of your rival, you can succeed in everything that you do just like your training knowledge of your tools and the nature of Evil can help you win the battle against it.

All kinds of fire extinguishing work on the basic principle of eliminating one of the elements of the Fire Triangle, Fuel, Heat and Oxygen that are necessary to sustain fire. If you can remove the fuel, the fire will die out. If you can cool the fire, it will diminish. If you can stop the oxygen source, it will suffocate and die.

Eradicating Evil requires a specialized skill set. However, adequate training can help staff and employees to handle fire before the experts arrive on the scene. The staff must be well acquainted with the fire risk assessment of their building, emergency procedures and know their responsibilities and duties. Fire Drills can help you and your staff to handle emergencies. They must be aware about Evacuation procedures, opening of exit doors, stopping of machines and isolating the power supply. They must also know all about the location and use of Fire Fighting equipment.

There are many kinds of Fire Fighting equipments that include different kinds of Fire Extinguishers, Fire Suppression systems, Water mists, Fire Alarms and several Fire Protection equipment including Hoses, Emergency Lighting and many more that workers and staff must know how to use.

Thus, knowledge of Fire and adequate training about Fire Safety measures, Prevention & Evacuation and Fire Extinguishing and Suppression Tools can help you to ensure Extinction of Fire Evil.

Fire is a savage Monster capable of great harm.

It can be eliminated only by courage and wisdom and the right tools because only the right tools can get the job done rightly!!

GENERAL PRECAUTIONS IN THE WORKPLACE

- Damaged electrical outlets, cords, cables, etc.

- Overloaded outlets and circuits

- Combustible objects in unsecured locations (included excessive trash and recycling)—keep these far from electrical equipment!

- Fire exit obstacles

  Keep workspace and equipment clean, dry, and well-ventilated, and especially clean of oil and dust.

Prepare for emergencies:

- Follow workspace protocol and guidelines to ensure safety and health; know and understand rules and procedures concerning fire emergencies.

- Ensure that smoke alarms and sprinkler systems are installed, working properly, and are not blocked.

- Conduct regular fire drills.

Employers should follow these tips:

- Post clear fire escape plans on every level.

- Educate all employees on emergency procedures, exit locations, escape routes, fire alarms and drills, and the use of fire extinguishers.

- Conduct regular drills.

- Install and properly maintain all fire safety equipments.

- Provide for disabled employees.

Hazardous electrics and equipment

Use only electrical products evaluated by a nationally recognized laboratory (*i.e.* UL).

Immediately replace damaged, hazardous equipment:

- Look out for anything that appears overheated, smells strange, or delivers electrical shock.

- Replace all damaged, worn, frayed, or old wires.

  Only use three-prong plugs in three-slot outlets (and, similarly: two-slot plug into two-slot outlets).

  Equipment that emanates substantial heat should be at least several feet away from combustible surfaces and objects.

- Heaters must include a thermostat control mechanism.

Smoke Alarms: A Necessity, not an Option

Invest smoke detectors for every room or office.

- Install dual sensor smoke alarms; make sure they contain both ionization and photoelectric smoke sensors.

  Test your smoke detectors (and sprinkling system) once a month.

  Replace the batteries at least once a year (possible exception: non-replaceable 10-year lithium batteries; still, be sure to test them); many manufacturers also encourage a replacement of the smoke detectors after a decade.

  Never disable a smoke alarm.

Consider smoke alarms for the disabled

- Audible alarms (pauses between the siren wail allow for auditory communication) are available for the visually impaired; visual alarms (with a flashing light or vibrating pad) are available for the hearing impaired.

A No-Smoking Zone is Less of a Danger Zone

Keep the workspace a no-smoking zone. If you must smoke, smoke outdoors, and always ensure that you properly extinguish the cigarette in a sand-filled can, or drown cigarette butts and ashes in water.

- Never throw away hot cigarette butts or ashes without attending to them properly.

  Be alert and then alert others. If you smell or spot fire or smoke, bring it immediately to attention.

  Never smoke where oxygen is being used; for instance, in a hospital room or hallway, or at a nursing home. Even if the oxygen is turned off, the building is much more vulnerable—oxygen can be explosive and will only serve to fan the flames.

In Case of Fire: Follow the Evacuation Plan

Immediately call 911 in case of a fire.

Know and understand the fire emergency and evacuation plan with these workplace fire safety tips:

- Plan at multiple escape routes from as many locations as possible.

- Check the condition of fire ladders and fire escapes; ladders should be collapsible and evaluated by a nationally recognized laboratory (*i.e.* UL); fire escapes need to be stable, secure, and easily accessible.

- Ensure that windows don't become obstacles; glass should be opened easily and screens should be swiftly removed.

Never use the elevator. Walk—don't run—down the stairs.

If you cannot evacuate,

- Remain calm and put as much distance as possible between yourself and the fire.

- Seal all cracks with wet materials (towels, jackets) to prevent smoke from seeping into the room.

- Wait at the window; shout for help and signal your location by waving the most visible object.

1) Open the window for air, but try not to break it; you may need to close it if smoke begins to seep in.

   Practise; can you feel your way out of the office and building with your eyes closed, or in the dark? Do you know multiple escape routes? Do you know the low windows from which you could jump? Do you instinctively use the back of your hand to feel a door's heat, and do you remain crouched down as close to the floor as possible?

RESIDENTIAL FIRE PREVENTION & SAFETY GUIDE

Time is of essence when it comes to fires at home. In just two short minutes, a fire can become life-threatening. In five minutes, an entire home can be engulfed in flames! Given the enormity of danger, it's important for residents and families to become familiar with how fireworks, the main causes of home fires, and the various methods for fire safety. Fire safety awareness has resulted in a lower number of fire deaths in past years, but the number is still pretty high, especially considering that residential fires are so preventable.

Staying safe from fires at home begins with you. Awareness alone is not enough; proper preventative action is crucial. Save your family from the trouble of having to deal with a fire at home, and a firefighter from risking his life running into your burning residence by taking action with our tips below.

A house fire is a disaster that is easily preventable. Every homeowner and family member should take the time to do the following to ensure fire safety. Losing your home to a fire is a scary thought, but there are plenty of things that you can do to stop a fire before it starts and keep your home and family safe.

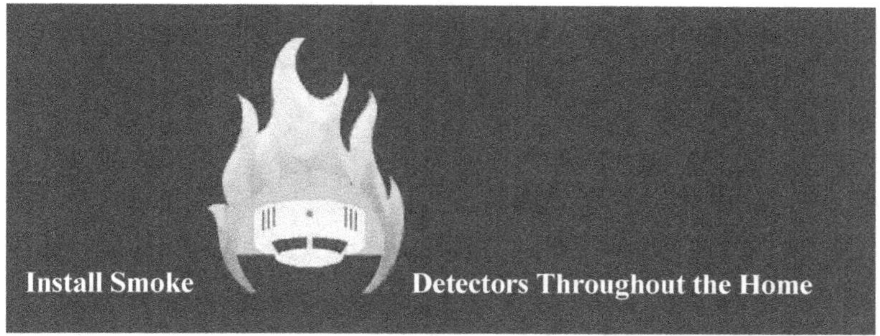

The first step for preventing a residential fire is properly installing enough smoke detectors throughout your home. Smoke detectors should be installed on every floor of your home and close to any bedrooms. Smoke detectors typically come standard in most home security systems. To make sure that the detectors are always in working order, you'll want to test them out once a month. Smoke detector manufacturers suggest that they should be completely replaced every 5 years. Do not disable any smoke detectors while cooking, as this can potentially result in tragedy. Though it's easy to forget such regular maintenance, but it's worth setting a reminder in your Smartphone's calendar to help you get it done. If they're not working, replace them immediately.

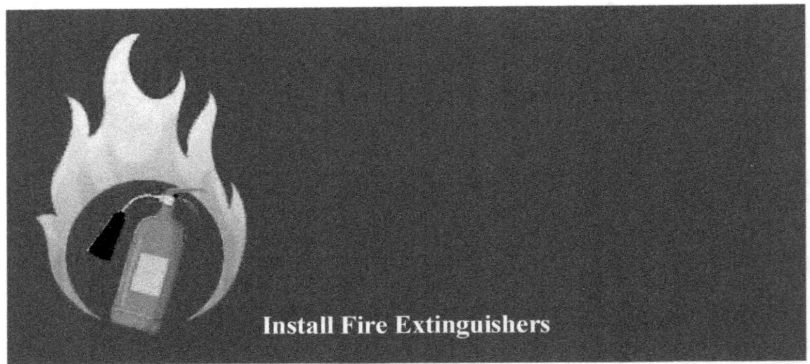

Once you've got the smoke detectors installed, it's time to make sure that you have fire extinguishers readily available throughout your residence. These will come in handy, should you experience a small fire. Using a fire extinguisher will prevent you and your family from having to battle a bigger fire. Fire extinguishers should be kept in the kitchen, garage, and any workshop areas of your home. Similar to smoke detectors, fire extinguishers should be checked regularly to ensure they are working properly. At the very least, keep one in the kitchen and others near high-risk areas like a fireplace. Remember to put the fire extinguisher far enough away from the potential fire source that you'll be able to grab it safely without getting too close to the stove or fireplace.

Regularly review the instructions and make sure that all members of the household know how to use the extinguisher properly. Post the P.A.S.S. acronym near the fire extinguisher:

P = Pull

A = Aim

S = Squeeze

S = Sweep

If you're not able to invest in fire extinguishers, a box of baking soda works in a pinch for grease fires.

Generously shake the baking soda over the grease fire to smother it.

If you are not sure about how to use a fire extinguisher, consider contacting your local fire department or contractor. You'll be able to learn how to properly use and maintain it.

Let's face it - kids are curious. This is a good and bad thing, but when it comes to something life-threatening like fire, curiosity can quickly turn into danger. Over 100,000 fires are set every year by kids under 5 years playing with lighters or matches. To avoid this from happening, it's essential to educate children about the potentially deadly consequences of playing with fire. Inform them to STOP, DROP, and ROLL if their clothes catch on fire in an emergency. Also, teach them about what firefighters do, and to not hide from them when they are in sight.

Having a well-thought out, organized plan is very important. Think about it—the last thing you want to do during a fire is to think rationally about what to do next to survive. Developing a plan for escape in advance will spare you some time (which is a huge deal during a fire).

Not only should you create a plan, you will also want to discuss it with your family members in detail so that everyone is on the same page, should a fire take place. The escape plan should include at least two escape routes from every bedroom. Everyone living at home should be familiar with basic home fire-safety procedures. This includes checking doors for heat before opening them, staying low on the ground to stay out of smoke, and knowing the closest way out. These little things can go a long way in saving lives during a blaze! Make digital copies of any valuable documents and records like birth certificates, and keep them in a safe place easily retrievable in case fire takes place.

In addition to creating a plan and talking about it, practise it. Fire drills are not only for grade school students-they're a good reminder for the people of almost all age groups.

On top of having a solid escape plan in place for yourself and your family, it's also crucial to make sure that everything at home is in working order. For example, windows should not be stuck, and if you have any window screens, they should be easily removed if need be. Do you want to use security bars? Make sure that they can be opened properly.

Have a Family Communications Plan Set

Got the escape plan out of the way? Now it's time to plan out your family communication methods. Firstly, make sure that everyone knows how to call 101. In any emergency, it's important to ensure that everyone at home knows who to contact if they are not able to locate one another, or in any other instance. Spend some time to speak with family members about who to call and where to meet in such cases, to be extra prepared.

Lastly, a medical alert system may be a great option for older adults to ensure that they are safe and able to communicate with emergency responders as well as loved ones.

Common Causes of Fire at Home

Avoid starting a fire by getting to know what often instigates flames at home:

Inspect heating sources

Regardless of what kind of primary heating you have in your home, an annual inspection will reduce your risk of fire.

Change furnace filters regularly to avoid a buildup of dust and lint that can easily catch fire. If you use space heaters, carefully inspect them before and after each use, and place them at least three feet away from anything combustible, such as fabric or paper. Check water heaters as well, especially those that run off gas and have a pilot light. Make sure that nothing is close to the heating element.

Lint will easily get a fire started under the right conditions, so it is very important to keep your clothing dryer well-maintained. It is highly recommended that the air exhaust pipe to the outside of the home be inspected yearly to ensure that there is no blockage, which may interfere with the dryer working efficiently and safely.

After each load, clear the lint filter before starting a new one. Check around the drum as well, because sometimes lint can get deposited in this area. If you can, avoid having your dryer operate overnight or while you are out of the house, keep in mind that it is better to do several rounds of drying if needed, rather than overloading the dryer. Doing so may lead to an excess of lint, increasing the chances of a house fire taking place.

To kids, fire is exciting and certainly peaks curiosity. It is very important that kids know about the serious dangers of fire. In addition to explaining how fire is a tool and not a toy, it's beneficial to also inform them of an escape plan, what the sound of the smoke alarm is like, etc. Keep them away from any stoves that are on or burning candles. Lighters and matches should not be left out in the open where children can easily access them.

Similarly, you can't expect pets at home to know any better. So, if any burning candles are left out in the open for them to reach or play with, you and your home may be in trouble.

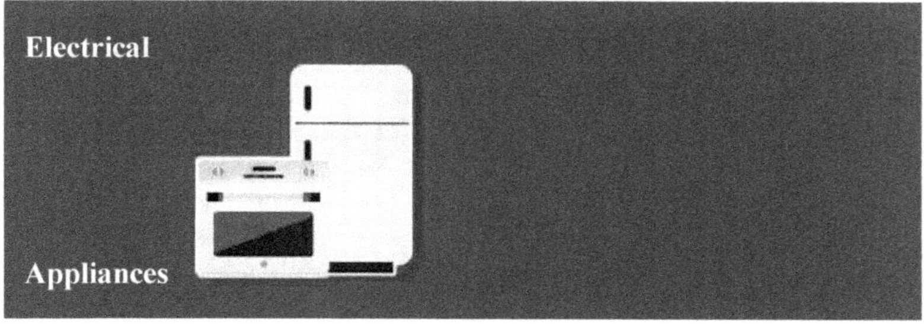

Faulty electrical appliances can also result in a fire, so it's imperative to check them regularly to make sure that they are operating properly. Frayed or damaged cords should be unplugged and replaced immediately. If you have kids at home, consider opting for tamper-resistant outlets, so that they don't injure themselves or pose a risk when you are not directly supervising. It is dangerous to constantly overload outlets with high-wattage devices, so it's strongly recommended that you spread out your appliances. As far as lighting goes, only use light bulbs that match the fixture's recommended wattage. Extension cords come in really handy when you need to plug in multiple devices in any given vicinity. Just make sure that they are not tucked in under rugs, carpet, or other furniture. Since they power so many things, it's inevitable that extension cords get hot and when overheated, it could fray or wear out, resulting in a potential fire hazard.

If you experience problems with any outlet or wiring at home often, such as blown fuse, constant light flickering, or sparking, then you may want to contact an electrician and have him address the issue. Putting this off may exacerbate the issue in the long run, and hence it's always better to tackle these problems as they arise.

Liquids like cleaning agents, paints, gasoline, and adhesives, for example, are highly flammable. This means that they can start fire with high temperatures or other sources like small sparks of static electricity. To prevent this from happening at home, store flammable liquids away from any heat source. If possible, keep it outside of the home in a ventilated and cool area.

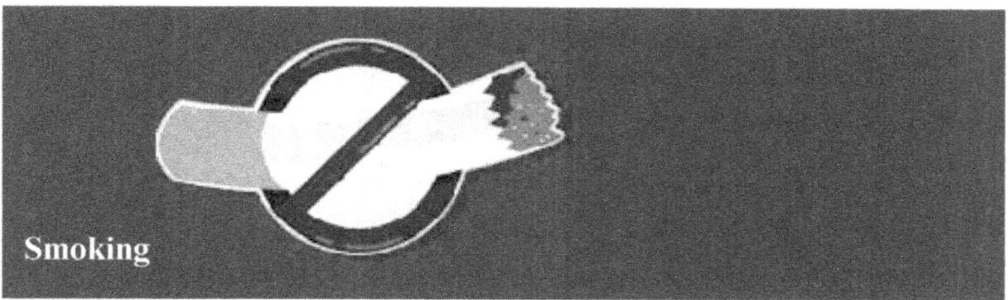

Another really common cause of house fire is smoking accidents. Smoking indoors is never a good idea. Take the extra step and go out onto your balcony or backyard if you must smoke. When you are done smoking, make sure that the embers are completely out in the ashtray or run under water.

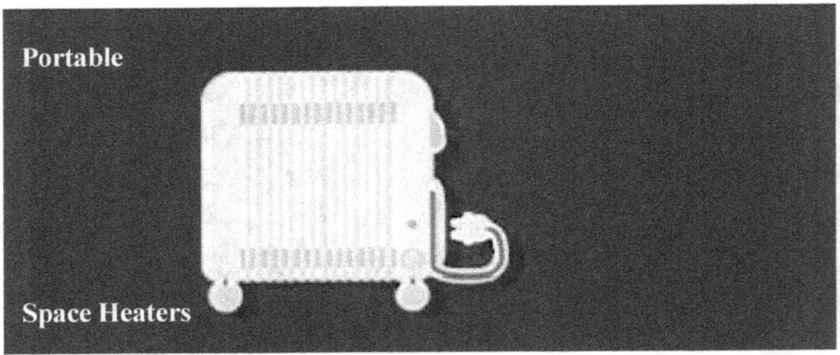

Space heaters come in really handy in the winter months when you only need to warm up one room, but it's important to use them responsibly. These actually account for a third of heating fire, so you will want to make sure that any flammable items are kept at least three feet away from an operating space heater. Keep the space heater on a flat and stable surface when using it so that it doesn't potentially fall on something and catch fire. Some are designed to automatically turn off once tipped over these ones are much safer. Space heaters should not be left on overnight or unattended.

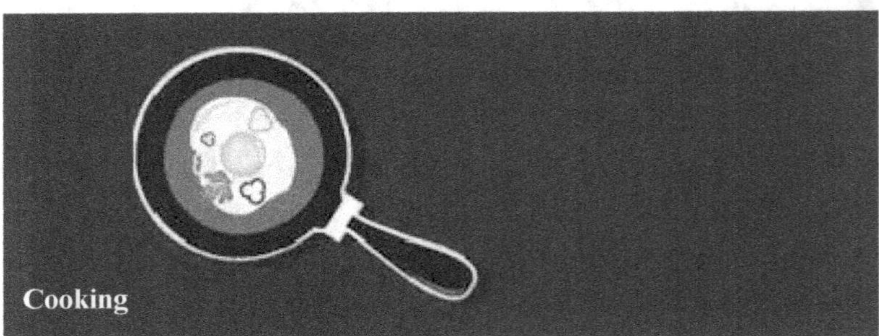

Most house fire occur as a result from using cooking oils, fryers, microwaves, and unattended cooking. To avoid potential hazards, never leave the kitchen unattended while cooking, especially when you are using high temperatures or cooking oil. After you are done with cooking, ensure that the stove and/or oven is completely turned off before leaving the kitchen. Hot items should be kept away from loose clothing, dish towels, and other fabrics that could potentially cause a fire.

Use a fireplace regularly at home? It is essential to get it checked out yearly to ensure that it is working properly. Similar to space heaters, you'll only want to use the fireplace when you are at home) and make sure that it's put out before you go to bed. To prevent flying sparks, utilize a fireplace screen big enough to cover the entire opening, and heavy enough to stop any rolling logs.

CONCLUSION

You might be thinking that these fire safety tips are common sense. However, it's easy to overlook them especially when busy and stressed about work, the holidays, and the likes. It's not uncommon that people lose track of even the most basic precautions. So, whether you're reading this piece to gain informational knowledge or to get a very much needed reminder, know that you can never play it too safe when it comes to fire prevention at home. Taking the necessary measures will not only save a ton of hassle and your precious belongings, but also your loved ones!

Next Step

For more details of fire safety equipments, risk assessments or fire safety training, you can log on to

manishkhatana.com or contact us

✉ at manish@palladiumss.com,

☎ or call me at 9971890006/01149025798

9 789390 116737